05/2005 $21.95   L.29.4

The Library of
ASTRONAUT BIOGRAPHIES™

GUS GRISSOM
The Tragedy of *Apollo 1*

Robert Greenberger

The Rosen Publishing Group, Inc., New York

Published in 2004 by The Rosen Publishing Group, Inc.
29 East 21st Street, New York, NY 10010

Copyright © 2004 by The Rosen Publishing Group, Inc.

First Edition

Library of Congress Cataloging-in-Publication Data

Greenberger, Robert.
Gus Grissom: the tragedy of *Apollo* 1/ by Robert Greenberger.— 1st ed.
   p. cm. — (The library of astronaut biographies)
Includes bibliographical references and index.
Contents: Finding his way—From top gun pilot to NASA recruit —Space training—Grissom and Liberty Bell 7—Gemini 3—An astronaut's last ride.
ISBN 0-8239-4458-1 (library binding)
1. Grissom, Virgil I.—Juvenile literature. 2. Astronauts—United States—Biography—Juvenile literature. [1. Grissom, Virgil I. 2. Astronauts.]
I. Title. II. Series.
TL789.85.G7G73 2004
629.45'0092—dc22
                                        2003011980

Manufactured in the United States of America

CONTENTS

INTRODUCTION	For All Humankind	**4**
CHAPTER 1	Finding His Way	**8**
CHAPTER 2	From Top Gun Pilot to NASA Recruit	**15**
CHAPTER 3	Space Training	**30**
CHAPTER 4	Grissom and *Liberty Bell 7*	**40**
CHAPTER 5	*Gemini 3*	**59**
CHAPTER 6	An Astronaut's Last Ride	**71**
CONCLUSION	A Pioneer's Legacy	**95**
GLOSSARY		**100**
FOR MORE INFORMATION		**103**
FOR FURTHER READING		**106**
BIBLIOGRAPHY		**108**
INDEX		**110**

FOR ALL HUMANKIND

I f we die, we want people to accept it. We're in a risky business, and we hope that if anything happens to us it will not delay the program. The conquest of space is worth the risk of life.

—Gus Grissom, responding to a reporter, at a 1969 press conference during preparations for the first manned Apollo mission, as quoted by the Associated Press

Lieutenant Colonel Virgil Ivan "Gus" Grissom did not have the flashiest personality among

Virgil "Gus" Grissom is seen through the window of the open hatch of his *Gemini 3* spacecraft on the morning of its March 23, 1965 launch.

the fabled Mercury 7 astronauts, nor was his work on the subsequent Gemini program the most important. And, yet, at the time of his death in a mission training accident, he was the Apollo program astronaut scheduled to become the first man on the Moon. In everything he did—as fighter pilot, test pilot, astronaut, and space engineer—Grissom distinguished himself with hard work, tireless energy, quiet determination, and simple humility.

Grissom worked hard to achieve his dreams, successfully realizing one goal after another, and was respected by those who worked alongside him for his thorough professionalism. He was also a loving husband and a good father to his two sons. In fact, right before his death, Grissom had just completed work on a book about the Gemini program entitled *Gemini!: A Personal Account of Man's Venture Into Space*. He intended it not only for his children but for all children of astronauts and those interested in manned space travel. He was trying to share the joy and wonder of his demanding work with the generations to come.

On the day he died, Grissom was eager to complete the Apollo test simulation in which he was taking part. Once the test was successfully completed, his Apollo space flight could be scheduled, and humans would get one step closer to the Moon. He wanted to not only expand his personal horizons by journeying to the Moon, but also to fulfill President John F. Kennedy's promise to the American public to put an American on the lunar surface by the end of the 1960s. It was an exciting time to be in the space program, a chance to see the world from a new and thrilling point of view.

It was also an exciting time to be an American as the country's high-altitude pioneers ventured into new frontiers and explored the unknown and the unseen. Throughout his life, Grissom desired to achieve the previously unachieved, to experience that which had never been experienced before. His determination to do so never weakened, and he would lose his life in this quest. Grissom's death, however, would make it possible for others to realize his dream of space exploration and discovery.

FINDING HIS WAY

When Virgil Ivan "Gus" Grissom was born on April 3, 1926, air travel was barely two decades old and was by no means a widespread form of transportation. No one in the Grissoms' tiny hometown of Mitchell, Indiana, imagined that one could make a living in the air, much less farther up in space.

The eldest of four children (including Norman, Lowell, and Wilma) born to Dennis and Cecile Grissom, Gus enjoyed his home life. Despite the Great Depression that had taken hold of the country three years after Gus's birth, Dennis Grissom managed to remain employed with the Baltimore and Ohio Railroad. The $24 weekly salary he earned as a signalman seemed sufficient to house and feed his family at 715 Baker Street. In fact, the family prospered as the years rolled by.

Gus was extremely intelligent. He had an IQ of 145 but still found school difficult. He did not develop a passion for any particular subject or activity. As quoted by IndianaHistory.org, Grissom said, "I guess it was a

This photograph shows Grissom at the age of ten. Though highly intelligent, he lacked interest in his studies.

case of drifting and not knowing what I wanted to make of myself. I suppose I built my share of model airplanes, but I can't remember that I was a flying fanatic."

Despite this sense of drift, Gus was a hard worker. To earn spending money, he became a paperboy. Every day he went to the local bus station to collect and then deliver the *Indianapolis Star* in

the morning and the *Bedford Times* in the afternoon. In the summer, he was hired by local growers to pick peaches and cherries in the orchards outside of town.

Gus's life suddenly became much more exciting when he began high school in 1940 and met fellow freshman Betty Moore. They caught each other's eye in the corridors or when he carried the flag onto the basketball court before games and she played drums in the school band. In his autobiography, Grissom wrote, "I met Betty Moore . . . and that was it, period, exclamation point! It was a quiet romance, as far as anyone could see, but a special closeness started then and has developed into something several light years beyond the power of mere words to describe."

An Enlisted Man

Gus's high school years passed uneventfully, but the world beyond Mitchell, Indiana, was shaken by World War II. The war's pull began to tug on the young man. As a high school senior, Gus received a year's training as an aviation cadet and decided to enlist in the armed forces. He had been considering this decision ever since Japan's 1941 surprise attack on the American fleet at Pearl Harbor—the event that had finally dragged the United States into the four-year-old war that was ravaging Europe and Asia. He received his orders in mid-1944 and joined the Army Air Force (which would become the United States Air Force in 1947). Grissom had begun to develop a keen interest in flying planes, and the army would provide him with an opportunity to take to the skies.

Grissom spent five weeks of basic training in Wichita Falls, Texas, but the war ended before he could receive any flight training. Joyous over the end of hostilities, Grissom was nevertheless disappointed that he had missed an opportunity to learn how to fly. Instead, he spent his remaining time in the army as a desk clerk at Brooks Field in San Antonio, Texas.

During a leave, on July 6, 1945, Grissom returned home to Mitchell to marry Betty Moore and begin a life together. From that day forward, the couple formed a unique and strong bond. They came to rely on each other and provide one another with rock-solid support in the years ahead.

Meanwhile, Grissom found himself assigned from one routine desk job to another. Knowing that he had joined the Army Air Force to fly fighter planes and not to type memos, he decided to leave the service. His discharge came through in November 1945. For the next year, Grissom drifted through a series of jobs, including installing school bus doors at Carpenter Body Works (the company in Mitchell, Indiana, that makes the yellow school buses used nationwide). Though busy, he still could not let go of his desire to fly.

A Dream of Flight

Finally, Grissom decided the best way to realize his dream of becoming an accomplished and talented pilot who knew his way around his aircraft was to go to college to study mechanical engineering. After discussing his options with Betty, Gus enrolled at Purdue University in West Lafayette, Indiana, in 1946.

The first semester was a difficult adjustment period for both Gus and Betty. Grissom and another student shared a basement apartment while Betty lived at home with her parents. To help

Gus Grissom as he appeared in the 1950 Purdue University yearbook *(inset)*. Above is Grissom Hall, in which Purdue's Aeronautical and Astronautical Engineering and Industrial Engineering departments are housed. The building was named in honor of Gus Grissom in 1967.

support her husband, Betty joined Gus for his second semester and worked as an operator for Indiana Bell Telephone. Grissom also got a job as a cook, working thirty hours a week in addition to his classes and homework.

Grissom did not take a break from school during summer vacations. He took additional courses instead. All of this hard work paid off. In

1950, he received a bachelor of science degree in mechanical engineering. Grissom could not savor this achievement for long, however. He needed to find a career. The recent graduate had to find a way to combine his need for work with his dream of flight.

CHAPTER 2

FROM TOP GUN PILOT TO NASA RECRUIT

In the years following the end of World War II, a new war broke out, but this was a very different sort of conflict. It became known as the Cold War—a long period of simmering tension and distrust between the United States and the Soviet Union (which is now Russia and several other former Soviet republics). Each nation tried to export its ideology to the other nations of the world. The United States tried to foster and protect democracy, while the Soviets advocated Communism. The two superpowers never actually fired a single shot at each other (hence, it was a "cold" war). However, they often supported and fought

The U2 spy plane, pictured above, was one of the high-tech jets developed by the United States during the Cold War with the Soviet Union. The high-altitude plane allowed American pilots to fly safely over Soviet territory and gather information on the enemy nation's weapons and missile programs.

with other nations' armies in conflicts—such as the Korean and Vietnam Wars. These conflicts often represented the struggle between democracy and Communism.

The Cold War required the superpowers to build and maintain large and high-tech arsenals of weapons for use in case actual war broke out between them. Fighter jets were an important part of this arsenal. As a result, it was a busy time for U.S. Air Force pilots.

More important, it was an exciting and daring time for test pilots who were risking their lives to help build the next generation of fighter jets and allow the United States to maintain its competitive edge over the Soviet Union. While Gus Grissom could have trained to become a pilot for the commercial airlines, he was far more drawn to the sense of adventure and national purpose represented by the air force pilots. Once again, he and Betty discussed their options as a team. They both decided that Gus should reenlist. An air force recruiting team happened to be visiting Purdue University at the time, so Grissom seized the opportunity.

Chasing MiGs in Korea

While Betty remained in Indiana, Gus was shipped back to Texas, this time to Randolph Air Force Base (AFB), and then on to Arizona's Williams AFB. During this period of training, Betty gave birth to their first son, Scott, an event Gus missed. He would not meet Scott until the

six-month-old and his mother finally joined Grissom in Arizona.

In March 1951, Grissom was promoted to second lieutenant, and the bump in salary took a lot of economic pressure off the growing family. This brief moment of comfortable togetherness was not to last long, however. In December, Grissom was shipped overseas to Korea as part of the 334th Fighter-Interceptor Squadron. They were stationed at Kimpo AFB, a mere twelve miles (19 kilometers) from the front lines. The Korean War (1950–1953) was a conflict in which armed forces of the United States and United Nations were defending South Korea from an invasion of the Communist forces of North Korea. American pilots flew many missions over North Korea trying to keep the skies clear of MiGs, warplanes provided by the Soviets to the Communist North Koreans. As his first experience with both flying and warfare, Korea was a thrilling and terrifying experience for Grissom.

One day, Grissom encountered his first North Korean MiG. He recounted the incident in the group memoir of the Mercury space program, *We Seven*: "I was flying along up there, and it was kind

Above is a portrait of Gus Grissom as a lieutenant in the air force. At top are four air force F-86 Sabrejets of the kind that Grissom flew during the Korean War. These fighter jets were some of the air force's most powerful weapons used against the Soviet-made MiGs flown by Communist North Korean pilots.

of strange. For a moment I couldn't figure out what those little red things were going by. Then I realized I was being shot at. I usually flew wing position in combat, to protect the flanks of other pilots and keep an eye open for any MiGs that might be coming across." Grissom later said, "I never did get hit, and neither did any of the leaders that I flew wing for."

In only six months, Grissom managed to successfully complete 100 combat missions, a great achievement for any pilot. Grissom was enjoying the experience and requested to stay on for an additional twenty-five missions, but his request was denied. He was shipped home in 1952 having earned two medals for his distinguished service in Korea.

Becoming a Test Pilot

Back in the United States, Grissom once again found himself having to decide what to do next with his life and career. Aerial combat in Korea had done nothing to dispel his passion for piloting. Flying was in his blood. One way he could maintain contact with the U.S. Air Force and draw a decent salary was to work as a flight instructor. Grissom soon began to work in this capacity at Bryan AFB (now closed) in Bryan, Texas. The job came just in time; in 1953, his second child, Mark, was born.

Grissom had found a job that allowed him to fly almost as much as he wanted. He loved the giddy sense of speed, altitude, and freedom that the jet planes gave him. Grissom racked up so many hours in the air that he quickly gained the admiration of his peers and became known as a "pilot's pilot."

Having logged so many flight hours, the next step for Grissom was to gain the training that would allow him to finally become a test pilot and achieve his longtime goal. Test pilots were very respected and dashing figures in the 1950s. In order to test the newest experimental fighter jets, they took enormous risks in unproven machines at great speeds and dizzying altitudes. Grissom wanted nothing more than to be a member of this select club.

In August 1955, Grissom enrolled at the Institute of Technology at Wright-Patterson Air Force Base in Dayton, Ohio. Upon completion of his training, he was then assigned to Wright-Patterson

Richard L. Johnson, chief test pilot at Edwards Air Force Base in 1955, shows off a new air force T-1 pressure suit. It includes oxygen hoses and a helmet microphone to protect the pilot in case of cabin pressure failure during flights. The inset shows an F-104 Starfighter of the sort tested by Gus Grissom in 1957.

AFB, but not before first meeting Gordon Cooper, who would later join the National Aeronautics and Space Administration's (NASA; a governmental agency committed to manned space flight and exploration) Mercury space program alongside Grissom. The two journeyed on for additional test pilot training at Edwards AFB in California.

Grissom received his test pilot certification in 1957 and was sent back to Wright-Patterson. There, he specialized in testing new jet fighters. "This was what I wanted all along," he said, as quoted in Betty Grissom and Henry Still's book, *Starfall*. "And when I finished my studies and began the job of testing jet aircraft, well, there wasn't a happier pilot in the Air Force."

The Space Race Is On

On October 4, 1957, while Grissom was testing the F-104 Starfighter, the Soviet Union launched *Sputnik*, the first human-made satellite to orbit Earth. This was the latest accomplishment in the one-upmanship going on between the United States and the Soviet Union during the Cold War.

THE RIGHT STUFF

It took a special brand of pilot to be willing to suit up and fly in a super-powerful but untested machine that had never been off the ground before. Test piloting became one of the glamour careers of the 1950s, and chief among this group of brave mavericks was Chuck Yeager. It was Yeager, flying the experimental X-51, who flew at supersonic speeds (faster than the speed of sound) for the first time in history. No one thought breaking the sound barrier was possible. Even Yeager had some moments of fear when the plane bucked as he neared supersonic speed. Once the sound barrier was passed, however, the airflow settled down, and Yeager was smoothly on his way, flying faster than any human had ever flown before.

Yeager's exploits were soon overshadowed by the space program, but the American public rediscovered him with the 1979 publication of

The Right Stuff, Tom Wolfe's historical novel about the Mercury 7—the first group of American astronauts who took part in the Mercury program. To accurately describe the dawn of the space era, Wolfe started by telling the stories of the test pilots, Yeager in particular. *The Right Stuff* made the Mercury 7 astronauts—who had been almost forgotten by a nation long distracted by Vietnam, the Watergate scandal, economic recession, and the Iran hostage crisis—celebrities all over again and once more turned Yeager into a national hero.

The extension of Cold War competition to space meant that the United States needed to start funneling a tremendous amount of money, time, and expertise into its own space program.

In 1958, President Dwight D. Eisenhower announced the creation of Project Mercury, a program designed to place a man in orbit around

In 1959, two years after the launch of the Soviet Union's *Sputnik*, the first satellite to be launched into orbit, Soviet premier Nikita Khrushchev *(center)* joins East Germany's Communist Party boss Walter Ulbricht *(left)* and East German premier Otto Grotewohl *(right)* beneath a model of the satellite in Leipzig, Germany.

Earth. The Mercury missions would require a new class of pilots—astronauts (a word whose Latin roots mean "travelers among the stars"). Eisenhower recommended that these new space pilots be drawn from the military ranks. There were no fliers better qualified for the danger and uncertainty of space travel than test pilots. The newly formed NASA further decided that its astronauts had to be less than forty years old, be shorter than 5'11" (to be able to fit in small, cramped space capsules), hold a bachelor degree or the equivalent in engineering, be a qualified jet pilot, be a graduate of test-pilot school, and have at least 1,500 hours of flying time.

NASA then asked the four branches of the armed services to provide a list of pilots who matched the criteria. The final list numbered nearly 500. After additional screening, 110 pilots were selected for more intensive study and testing.

Grissom was one of the pilots who appeared on the list of candidates. One day, he received a message containing top-secret orders, summoning him to Washington, D.C. He was to report in civilian dress, not his air force uniform. It was all very mysterious and intriguing. Even Grissom's superiors had no idea what it was all about. As Grissom said in *Gemini!*, "On the appointed day, wearing my best civilian suit, and still as baffled as ever, I turned up at the Washington address I'd been given . . . I was convinced that somehow or other I had wandered right into the middle of a James Bond novel."

Grissom was one of nearly four dozen people brought into a meeting room for a NASA presentation on Project Mercury. Chatting with the other somewhat bewildered men, Grissom quickly discovered that they were all test pilots. When the presentation began, Project Mercury and its goals were explained to the pilots. It became clear that NASA was hoping to find men willing to leap into the great unknown of space travel. The attendees were told that their participation would be entirely voluntary. This was not a military program; no one was going to be ordered to take part in Mercury. As the presentation continued, Grissom instinctively knew that the next great frontier was no longer supersonic jet travel, but journeys to the stars. He wanted to be on the leading edge of that frontier and knew before the meeting was over that he would volunteer for the program.

So many pilots from this first session volunteered that the remaining pilots on the list were dismissed. As Grissom recalled in *We Seven*, "I did not think my chances were very big when I saw some of the other men who were competing for the team. They were a good group, and I had a lot of respect for them. But I decided to give it the old school try and to take some of NASA's tests." It would be one of the most important decisions of his life, one that would lead to unprecedented triumph and unimaginable tragedy.

CHAPTER 3

SPACE TRAINING

Grissom and the other thirty-eight volunteers reported to Lovelace Clinic at
Wright-Patterson for extensive astronaut
testing. Additional studies, including underwater
pressure-suit tests, heat tests, acceleration tests, and
vibration tests, were conducted at the Aeromedical
Laboratory of the Wright Air Development Center
in Ohio. Since astronautics was such a new field, the
scientists and doctors had no points of comparison
against which to test the volunteers. As a result, they
dreamt up every imaginable physical and psycholog-
ical test to try to separate those who seemed likely

to perform well in the potentially stressful conditions of space from those who might "crack" physically or emotionally. The battery of tests was grueling, exhausting, and extremely uncomfortable. None of the candidates enjoyed the experience, and some dropped out of the program.

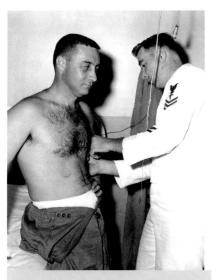

Gus Grissom has sensors attached to his body before a session in a centrifuge during astronaut training.

As the weeks wore on, Grissom found some of the tests downright bizarre and truly hated the psychiatric exams. As he put it in *Gemini!*, "I tried not to give the headshrinkers [psychiatrists] anything more than they were actually asking for. At least, I played it cool and tried not to talk myself into a hole. I did not have the slightest idea what they were trying to prove, but I tried to be honest with them . . . without getting carried away and elaborating too much."

The original Mercury 7 astronauts are shown during training at NASA's Langley Research Center in Virginia in March 1961. From left are Scott Carpenter, Gordon Cooper, John Glenn, Gus Grissom, Wally Schirra, Alan Shepard, and Deke Slayton.

His responses must have impressed someone because on April 13, 1959, Captain Grissom received word that he would be one of the Mercury 7 astronauts. Joining him would be Lieutenant Malcolm Scott Carpenter, U.S. Navy; Captain Leroy Gordon Cooper Jr., U.S. Air Force; Lieutenant Colonel John Herschel Glenn Jr., U.S. Marine Corps; Lieutenant Commander Walter Marty "Wally" Schirra Jr., U.S.

Navy; Lieutenant Commander Alan Bartlett Shepard Jr., U.S. Navy; and Captain Donald Kent "Deke" Slayton, U.S. Air Force.

With the selection of the Mercury 7, the astronaut training began in earnest. Once accepted into the space program, Grissom asked his family to relocate yet again. Now they would set up home near Langley AFB in Virginia, where the astronauts continued to train.

In addition to training, the astronauts took a very active interest in the design of the Mercury space capsules. They felt it was extremely important that they fully understand the vehicle that would carry them out of Earth's atmosphere and back again. In order to familiarize themselves with the capsule's design and provide feedback, the astronauts crossed the country to meet with manufacturers, engineers, scientists, and government officials. The seven astronauts worked closely with NASA engineers and aerospace contractors to help figure out how to build a space capsule that could be shot into orbit and return safely to Earth. The seven men split up specialized duties, depending on their areas of expertise, or special knowledge.

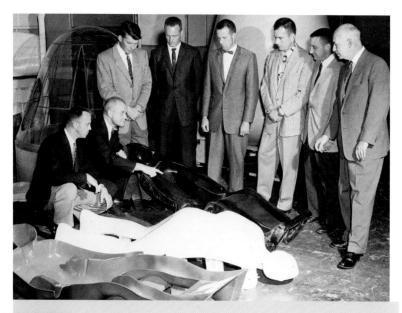

The Mercury 7 astronauts inspect plastic molds of the couch-type seats that will be installed in Mercury capsules. From left are Alan Shepard, John Glenn, Wally Schirra, Scott Carpenter, Gordon Cooper, Deke Slayton, Gus Grissom, and Project Mercury director Robert Gilruth.

Putting his engineering degree to good use, Grissom went to work on the capsule's automatic and manual controls. The astronauts and engineers would meet regularly and share notes, so everyone had a chance to see beyond their immediate tasks and get an idea of how the entire project was developing. Once the first year of training was complete, Grissom stopped to figure out how long he had been on the road. The result of his calculation—305 out of the last 365 days away from home—astonished him.

During the second year of training, NASA announced the Mercury program's flight order. The order in which astronauts would be sent into space on the seven planned Mercury space flights reflected in part how they were ranked by NASA. The first up were among the best of the group. Grissom was pleased to learn that he was scheduled to make the second planned flight, behind Alan Shepard. It somehow made the sixteen-hour days feel even more worthwhile.

The First American in Space

As work on the Mercury program continued, the Soviets once more trumped America by sending Yuri Gagarin and *Vostok 1* into space on April 12, 1961. He became the first human ever to leave Earth's atmosphere and complete a full orbit of the planet. It was a stunning triumph for the Soviet Union. The resulting pressure placed on NASA and its pilots to catch up to the Soviets became even more intense.

MERCURY, GEMINI, AND APOLLO

The major goal of the first Mercury flights was simply to launch one man into space and get him home safely. It included a series of space flights designed to put manned space capsules in orbit around Earth and test the technology and techniques that would eventually put a man on the Moon. The Gemini missions were designed to refine the technology and techniques required for the Moon landings that were scheduled to take place in the later Apollo missions. The Gemini program had four major goals: to subject two astronauts and their equipment to long-duration flights; to rendezvous and dock with other orbiting vehicles; to perfect reentry methods and landing at a preselected point; and to gain information about weightlessness and its effect on astronauts.

Each program was built upon and further developed the achievements of the previous one. In turn, Gemini provided valuable stepping stones for the Apollo missions and an eventual Moon landing.

Less than a month later, on May 5, America responded by sending Shepard into the skies aboard *Freedom 7*. The mission was known as *Mercury-Redstone 3* (MR-3; Redstone referred to the rocket that would carry the capsule into space). MR-3 was a suborbital flight, meaning that Shepard briefly left Earth's atmosphere but did not orbit the planet before returning and splashing down in the Atlantic Ocean. Basically, his capsule was shot high into Earth's atmosphere, reached a peak height, and fell back down, in an arclike trajectory, or flight path. It was a great feat for NASA and the United States. They had sent the first American into space. Nevertheless, many people felt it was a minor achievement compared to *Vostok 1*'s orbital flight.

Many Americans, including politicians, demanded that NASA match the Soviets' feat, but the space agency remained cautious and methodical, sticking to its carefully scheduled program in which each space flight built upon the successes of the previous one and tested the technology and techniques required for the next one. Grissom's flight—designed to further establish that humans could be put into space—would be used to prove Shepard's success was

not a fluke. It was essential to prove that not only would the United States catch up in the race with the Soviets, but it would also soon win it and come to dominate space.

Grissom's Mercury Mission

The specific goals of Grissom's space flight, *Mercury-Redstone 4* (MR-4), were to familiarize astronauts with a brief but complete space flight experience. This would include liftoff and its heavy load of gravitational forces (G-forces), a brief period of weightlessness, the stress and dangers of reentry (during which the capsule shakes violently and is dangerously heated when passing back through Earth's dense atmosphere), and splashdown and retrieval, or pickup of the astronaut and his capsule. During the flight, NASA wanted to test how well an astronaut could function in space and perform specific tasks, such as operating manual spacecraft controls and maintaining voice communication with ground control. This would also allow NASA to study how space flight, particularly weightlessness, affects the human body. Finally, successful use of the new explosive hatch was a top priority for MR-4.

Astronaut trainees experience a brief period of weightlessness onboard a C-135 transport plane. This plane makes a series of steep climbs and sudden dives that create conditions similar to zero gravity for about half a minute. This lets trainees practice how to move their bodies and manipulate tools in space.

What had been learned from Shepard's and Grissom's space flights would allow the succeeding Mercury astronauts to make the next leap forward—extended missions beyond Earth's atmosphere and in orbit around the planet. Eventually, Grissom's pioneering work would also help put an American on the Moon.

CHAPTER 4

GRISSOM AND
LIBERTY BELL 7

As the date for his mission came closer, Grissom began taking fewer physical risks. He did not want anything to jeopardize his participation on MR-4. His main form of exercise was water skiing, but in the interests of safety, he decided to curtail that, and began paying more attention to the speed limit signs on the highways throughout Florida.

Grissom's capsule, number 11, was delivered to Cape Canaveral on March 7, 1961, and 136 days later, it was ready for launch. In the meantime, the craft was opened up so pieces could be removed and tested individually. They were then reinstalled so tests of the capsule's various systems—such as electrical, communication, environmental (climate control), and control/steering—could be performed. Grissom was present much of the time, making sure he was comfortable with the work being performed and the capsule's progress.

Final Tests

Grissom's capsule, *Liberty Bell 7*, was placed atop the Redstone rocket on June 1, in preparation for the launch that was scheduled for eighteen days later. Grissom then spent the next two and a half weeks observing or participating in the testing of every system to make sure the launch would go off flawlessly. In *We Seven*, Grissom said, "During this time I became familiar with the launch procedure and grew to know and respect the launch crews. I gained confidence in their professional approach and in the smooth way they executed the prelaunch tests."

NASA ran a complete launch drill on July 7 to test radio frequency compatibility, ensuring that no radio signals interfered with one another and no

Technicians from NASA's Langley Research Center construct a prototype, or early experimental version, of the Mercury capsule. These capsules, designed for unmanned flight and known as "Little Joe," were a separate design from the Mercury capsules that eventually went into space.

stray frequency would accidentally activate any of the spacecraft's systems. Grissom suited up and was driven to the capsule at T minus 170 (170 minutes to launch). He entered the capsule at T minus 123 as scheduled and powered it up by turning on all the instruments.

Grissom declared himself satisfied with the capsule and said that everything should proceed as planned. When he left Cape Canaveral to go home for the weekend, he asked the engineers not to tinker with anything. Everything was already perfect.

Soaring into Space

The launch of *Mercury-Redstone 4* was scheduled for July 18, 1961. Grissom's patience would be tested, however, when the flight was postponed twice due to bad weather. On the second attempt, on July 19, Grissom was within ten minutes of takeoff before the decision was made to scrub the launch. Each time, he got suited up (an hours-long process), was medically checked out, ate a steak breakfast, and was cleared to fly. Each time, however, cloud cover and poor weather scrapped the flight. After the second postponement, the launch was rescheduled for July 21.

On that day, Grissom awoke at 1:10 AM. He had a breakfast and was pronounced fit to fly despite being tired and having a slightly sore throat. At 4:00 AM, Grissom entered *Liberty Bell 7*. The countdown proceeded fairly smoothly, with one planned hour-long hold called to evaluate weather conditions.

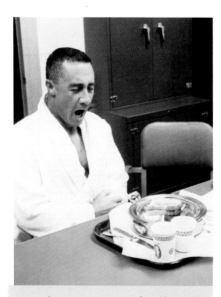

On the morning of July 19, 1961, Gus Grissom yawns over his breakfast. His Mercury spaceflight would be postponed due to bad weather.

Several glitches did pop up, however. At T minus 45 minutes, a thirty-minute hold was called to fix a faulty hatch bolt. At T minus 30 minutes, a nine-minute hold was called to turn off the searchlights on the launchpad that might possibly interfere with the radio transmission of crucial data between the capsule and mission control during the launch. Just fifteen minutes before the launch, a forty-one-minute hold on the countdown was called to await better cloud conditions. During all these delays—for three hours and twenty-two minutes—Grissom sat in the confines of *Liberty Bell* 7 and waited patiently with a growing sense of excitement.

After the clouds cleared, the countdown was resumed at T minus 15 minutes. There would be no further interruptions. After the many long weeks of training, testing, and tinkering, the launch finally went off, without a hitch. Grissom was soaring into the skies, as the G-forces topped out at 11.2 (eleven times the force of gravity felt on Earth). This did not bother Grissom a bit because he had been subjected to as many as 16 Gs in preparation for launch. At the peak of his capsule's arclike trajectory, Grissom experienced five minutes and eighteen seconds of weightlessness. Since he was tightly strapped into his seat and was not moving around the cramped capsule, he did not experience the full sensation of weightlessness that later Apollo astronauts would feel during their extended flights in roomier capsules.

Grissom was a little bothered by the sluggish response of the capsule's attitude controls (the instruments that help keep the capsule oriented toward a specific reference point, such as a star, the Moon, Earth, or the horizon). Whereas Alan Shepard could control movement of one of the capsule's axes at a time (up and down or side to side) on MR-3, Grissom worked with NASA engineers to allow him to control more than one axis at a time. The controls functioned slowly, however, and Grissom spent more time than provided for getting

The liftoff of *Mercury-Redstone 4* on July 21, 1961, would carry Gus Grissom and his *Liberty Bell 7* capsule into space for a fifteen-and-a-half-minute suborbital flight. This was NASA's second manned spaceflight and helped prove that the United States was catching up in the space race with the Soviet Union.

manual control over the craft. The yaw (side-to-side movement) was tried first, followed by the pitch (up and down). Grissom overshot his marks, costing him valuable time. This meant a planned roll of the capsule had to be dropped from the flight plan. The automated systems worked fine, however, although they burned fuel at a faster rate than expected. Later, Grissom said more time in the simulator would have helped him work more quickly and efficiently.

Grissom's time in space would be very brief. The entire flight lasted only fifteen minutes and thirty-seven seconds. He would travel a distance of 302 miles (486 km) and reach a height of 118 miles (190 km) above Earth. Though the mission was brief and had modest aims, it had accomplished its goal: NASA established to itself and the world that it knew how to place a man in space and get him home safely.

Splashdown into Controversy

It was soon time to return to Earth. After an uneventful reentry, the capsule deployed its parachutes and

landed in the Atlantic Ocean, just three miles (4.8 km) away from its intended target, and 302 miles (486 km) east of the launch site at Cape Canaveral. The precisely executed splashdown was a testament to Grissom's skillful control of the capsule.

While waiting for a helicopter to retrieve him and his capsule, however, something happened that blackened Grissom's reputation for years and marred an otherwise successful mission. As he was going through his postflight checklist, recording instrument readings with a grease pencil, three helicopters approached. He radioed to them that he needed five more minutes to complete his work before leaving the capsule.

In *We Seven*, Grissom described what happened next: "I opened up the faceplate on my helmet, disconnected the oxygen hose from the helmet, unfastened the helmet from my suit, released the chest strap, the lap belt, the shoulder harness, knee straps, and medical sensors. And I rolled up the neck dam of my suit . . . According to the plan, the pilot was to inform me as soon as he had lifted me [the capsule] up a bit so that the capsule would not ship

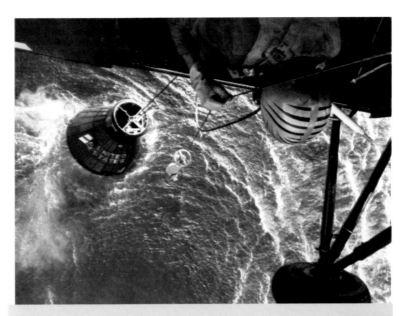

As *Liberty Bell 7* takes on water and begins to sink, a navy recovery helicopter lowers a cable toward the capsule in an attempt to pull it out of the water. The flooded capsule was too heavy for the helicopter to lift, and it had to be cut loose and left to sink beneath the waves.

water when the hatch blew. Then I would remove my helmet, blow the hatch and get out."

He then heard what he described as a dull thud, and the hatch suddenly blew, shearing itself off from the capsule. With ocean water pouring in, Grissom had no choice but to exit the capsule. In the rush, however, he forgot to close the seals on his flight suit

that would allow it to retain air, allowing him to float. Things quickly went from bad to worse. Once in the ocean, he got tangled in the capsule's parachute lines and fought desperately to free himself. Once he did, he began to swim away.

One of the helicopters soon arrived, hooked a recovery line to the now-flooded *Liberty Bell 7*, and

The top of *Liberty Bell 7* can still be seen above the waves moments before it sinks to the ocean floor. An explosive hatch that may have detonated too early may have been to blame. The triumph of Gus Grissom's Mercury spaceflight was overshadowed by this accident.

tried to lift it out of the water. Because it was flooded, however, the capsule had become extremely heavy. The helicopter's warning lights began flashing, indicating that the strain was too great for the helicopter's engines. Pilot Jim Lewis cut the line and reluctantly let the space capsule sink 15,000 feet (4,572 m) to the ocean floor.

Meanwhile, Grissom was struggling to stay afloat, his efforts made more difficult by the water now being churned up by the whirring of the helicopter's blades. Another helicopter arrived on the scene and lowered a horse collar for him. Once secured to it, Grissom was raised aboard. Though relieved to be out of the ocean, he was upset and angry, watching in anguish as the capsule sank beneath the waves.

Once on the aircraft carrier USS *Randolph*, Grissom spoke on the phone with President John F. Kennedy, who was pleased his fellow American was still alive. "It was especially hard for me as a professional pilot," Grissom recalled later in *We Seven*. "In all of my years of flying—including combat in Korea—this was the first time that my aircraft and I had not come back together. In

my entire career as a pilot, *Liberty Bell* was the first thing I had ever lost."

Gus called Betty after arriving at Grand Bahama Island for debriefing. She helped lighten his mood by joking that she heard he got a little wet. Grissom tried to focus on what had been accomplished during his extremely successful mission and not let the concluding mishap sour it all. The misfired hatch, however, cast a cloud of failure over MR-4. As far as the public knew, something had gone wrong and Grissom had let his capsule sink.

Looking back on the incident, there remain two interpretations of what actually happened: either Grissom, a normally calm and relaxed man, panicked and activated the detonating fuse too early, thereby flooding his capsule, or the untested hatch blew on its own and Grissom did what he had to do by escaping the sinking *Liberty Bell*. Most NASA engineers now say the second scenario is the more likely.

After returning to Patrick AFB at Cape Canaveral, Grissom was reunited with his family, and NASA head James Webb presented Grissom with a Distinguished Service Medal. This flush of success

A crowd of New Yorkers gathers in the Chrysler Building to watch a live broadcast of Gus Grissom's Mercury spaceflight. This tremendous public interest and enthusiasm turned more critical when Gus Grissom faced relentless questioning about his lost Mercury capsule following his return to Earth.

and cheer was quickly dampened by lingering doubts about the blown hatch. At a press conference following his return, Grissom was irritated by the relentless questions that focused on the lost capsule rather than the flight's accomplishments.

A NASA committee was assembled to study what went wrong. After it completed its investigation, astronaut Wally Schirra stated that there was

LIBERTY BELL RESCUED

Liberty Bell 7 was thought to be lost forever when it sank in 1961. Instead, on July 20, 1999, it was located by Curt Newport, a salvage expert. He had spent the last fourteen years searching for the capsule and managed to find it with funding from the Discovery Channel, a cable channel devoted to scientific and nature programming.

Newport used sonar in the general area of the capsule's splashdown and detected something deep beneath the waves that he thought might be the Liberty Bell. His hunch was correct, and he set about raising the capsule. Once recovered, it was cleaned and restored. In it were some of Grissom's gear and a collection of Mercury dimes he had taken up with him to bring back as souvenirs. After being spruced up, *Liberty Bell 7* went on a three-year tour around America and was then put on permanent display at the Kansas Cosmosphere and Space Center, the institution responsible for the capsule's restoration.

The reappearance of *Liberty Bell 7* provided a long overdue opportunity to celebrate Grissom's achievement, integrity, and grit. At the public unveiling, Jim Lovell, the astronaut made famous by his grace and ingenuity under extreme pressure during the nearly disastrous *Apollo 13* mission, told DiscoveryChannel.com, "The exhibit gives you a sense of what Gus was all about . . . a tremendous patriot."

Max Ary, of the Kansas Cosmosphere and Space Center, told Jim Banke of Space.com, "It puts Gus Grissom in the right perspective. Gus was one of our great astronauts, and I don't think he got his just due. And I hope that as this exhibit travels around the country, he is going to be remembered for who he was, and that was truly one of our great space pioneers."

The recovered *Liberty Bell 7* capsule at the Kansas Cosmosphere and Space Center

no evidence to indicate that Grissom panicked. Instead, it seemed as if the hatch blew on its own. One of the pieces of evidence that supported this conclusion came from a test of the explosive hatch device. Manually detonating the fuse would require an enormous amount of strength and would leave the hands bruised. Grissom had no such bruises. As quoted by TheSpacePlace.com, Schirra concluded, "There was only a very remote possibility that the plunger could have been actuated inadvertently by the pilot." A cloud of public doubt and suspicion lingered, however.

Moving Forward

In subsequent years, a variety of NASA personnel spoke out in favor of the accident theory, including Sam Beddingfield, an engineer responsible for the recovery system on the Mercury capsule, and Guenter Wendt, the man who helped Grissom board the capsule. Wendt believes that the MDF (mild detonating fuse) was accidentally activated from the outside when a parachute hatch opened during the main parachute deployment.

Gus Grissom is reunited with his family at Patrick Air Force Base in Florida following his return from space aboard the *Mercury-Redstone 4* mission. Angered and frustrated by the loss of *Liberty Bell 7*, Gus's family was a great comfort to him as he weathered a storm of questions and criticism.

Despite the mishap and the resulting cloud of suspicion, Grissom remained in the space program, receiving his astronaut wings for the achievements of the Mercury flight on December 7, 1961. The following July, he was promoted to the rank of air force major. By then, Grissom had succeeded in putting MR-4 behind him. He began looking forward to the next phase of NASA's space

program—Gemini—a series of missions designed to test the technology and techniques required to put men on the Moon in the later Apollo missions. Not wanting to be left out, Grissom set his sights on earning a seat on a new space flight.

The Gemini program would offer Gus Grissom a chance to redeem himself in the public eye and prove that he was among NASA's very best, most talented and competent astronauts. The boost he would receive from Gemini, however, would also set him on a path toward tragedy.

CHAPTER 5

GEMINI 3

Gus Grissom had traveled through Earth's atmosphere into space and returned. His successful journey paved the way for the even more ambitious orbital missions of the later Mercury space flights. This was no time to bask in his achievement, however. Instead, Grissom was already planning his return to space.

As he recalled in *Gemini!*, "When my Mercury flight aboard the *Liberty Bell* capsule was completed, I felt reasonably certain, as the program was planned, that I wouldn't have a second [Mercury] space flight. By then Gemini was in the

This is NASA's official logo for the Gemini project, a series of two-man space flights.

works, and I realized that if I were going to fly in space again, this was my opportunity, so I sort of drifted unobtrusively into taking more and more part in Gemini."

Fellow astronaut Wally Schirra agreed when speaking to AirSpaceMagazine.com: "When Gus finished his Mercury flight, he knew he was out of the loop because we had to go through the seven [Mercury astronauts] and he looked at it and said, 'My God, we are not going to have that many [Mercury] flights! I'm going to go up to St. Louis and play with Gemini.' So it was essentially his spacecraft. He practically had it to himself."

Building a Spacecraft

Given his engineering degree and spaceflight experience, Grissom was the perfect astronaut to get into the nitty-gritty of building the next generation

ASA-S-65-893

This is an artist's conception of the two-man Gemini spacecraft in flight. Grissom played a major role in the design and development of this very successful capsule. It was a fully maneuverable craft that allowed astronauts to be true pilots, as they controlled its course in orbit and during reentry and landing.

space vehicle. The Gemini capsules were being designed to give astronauts greater maneuvering control over the spacecraft—letting them be pilots, not merely passengers. Unlike Mercury capsules, which were basically catapulted into space and fell back down, the Gemini craft were built to be fully functional and responsive spaceships. They were to be two-man, extended mission spacecraft that

THE IMPORTANCE OF A NAME

Even in the midst of rigorous training for the upcoming *Gemini 3* mission, Grissom gave some thought to naming his spacecraft. He initially wanted to call it *Wapasha*, after a Native American tribe that hailed from his home state of Indiana. It was pointed out to Grissom that the press would dub the ship the *Wabash Cannonball*, in reference to a popular train of the time. Since the *Wabash* ran on a train line competing with his father's Baltimore and Ohio line, Grissom abandoned it. At the time, a popular musical was playing on Broadway, *The Unsinkable Molly Brown*, about a survivor of the doomed Titanic ocean liner. Grissom decided to deal with the press criticism of the loss of the *Liberty Bell 7* through humor; he wanted to name his spacecraft the *Molly Brown*. NASA did not appreciate the joke and requested a substitute name. When Gus offered *Titanic* instead, NASA reluctantly accepted *Molly Brown*.

would be fully maneuverable by the astronauts in orbit and controlled by them during reentry and landing. As a result, Grissom's experience with the various manual controls of *Liberty Bell 7* allowed NASA engineers to improve the flexibility and positioning of the Gemini controls. As fellow astronaut Deke Slayton wrote in *Deke!*, "Gemini would not fly without a guy at the controls . . . It was laid out the way a pilot likes to have the thing laid out . . . Gus was the guy who did all that."

Grissom was soon flying from one manufacturer to another, personally supervising each element in the Gemini program. It got so people took to nicknaming the craft the Gusmobile. NASA could not have been happier having one of its own astronauts so dedicated to the program and providing such invaluable expertise. As a result, Grissom had assured himself a place aboard a Gemini mission, even though the second wave of astronauts—those who were accepted into the space program after the original Mercury 7—were completing their training, eagerly awaiting their turn on the flight schedule.

Joining him on the Gemini flight would be John W. Young, the first of the new crop of astronauts.

This is a 1964 portrait of the *Gemini 3* prime and backup crews wearing their full pressure suits. Portable air conditioners pumped cool air through hoses into the suits. From left to right are John Young and Gus Grissom, *Gemini 3*'s prime crew, and Wally Schirra and Thomas Stafford, the backup crew.

Young had been a test pilot for the navy and an aeronautical engineer. Grissom noted that the training for Gemini was much harder than that for his Mercury flight. The equipment was much more complex and required far more time to master. He also no longer had the luxury of working alone and in peace. He had to form a good and close working relationship with Young, since they would share tight quarters both in the testing mockup on Earth and in the actual craft up in space.

The only thing standing between Grissom and a return to space were the first two Gemini missions. These were unmanned missions employing a robotic "crew." *Gemini 2*, in particular, suffered numerous delays, causing Grissom and Young great frustration. It was finally launched successfully on January 19, 1965, with everything going by the book. *Gemini 3* now could be scheduled for a launch on March 23, 1965.

Getting the Job Done

Liftoff of *Gemini 3* on March 23, 1965, ushered in a new era for NASA, and the mission could not have gone better. It was a relatively simple four-hour and fifty-three-minute flight that would orbit Earth three times. It was designed to test the kind of spacecraft maneuverability that would be crucial to later Gemini flights and the eventual Moon shots of the Apollo program. NASA needed to determine how well astronauts could control and maneuver a vehicle in space.

Maneuverability would be the key to the capsule docking technology required for Moon landings. In a lunar mission, a lunar lander must separate from the main orbiting space capsule to journey to the Moon and safely reattach itself to the orbiter at the conclusion of its mission before returning to Earth.

Command pilot Gus Grissom is seen sitting in the Gemini capsule, preparing it for the launch of the *Gemini 3* spaceflight. This photograph was taken just moments before the hatches were closed and secured, sealing Grissom and fellow astronaut John W. Young in the *Molly Brown*.

The *Molly Brown* performed beautifully. In *Gemini!*, Grissom said, "To our intense satisfaction, we were able to carry out these maneuvers almost exactly as planned. The longer we flew, the more jubilant we felt. We had a really fine spacecraft, one we could be proud of in every respect."

At the end of the *Molly Brown*'s third orbit, the astronauts decreased the capsule's altitude using manual controls and fired retro-rockets that would propel them back into Earth's atmosphere to begin reentry. Splashdown occurred in the Atlantic Ocean, near Grand Turk Island, at 2:16 PM. Because the spacecraft did not experience as much lift as expected during reentry, it landed almost seventy miles (112.7 km) off course. This meant Grissom and Young would have a lengthy wait for retrieval by either aircraft carrier or helicopter.

When the craft splashed down, Grissom saw that his window was below the water. He had not released the opened parachute from the capsule after splash-down, and now the wind was tugging the chute along with a half-submerged spacecraft in tow. Grissom released the parachute, and the capsule quickly righted itself. While waiting for pickup, however, the

John Young sits in a life raft waiting to be picked up by a navy recovery helicopter following the successful splashdown of *Gemini 3* on March 23, 1965. Navy swimmers in an inflatable boat can be seen to the left as they near Young.

inside of the craft grew extremely hot, and the rocking of the waves made the men seasick. "*Gemini* may be a good spacecraft, but she's a lousy ship," Grissom later noted, as quoted in Peter Bonds's *Heroes in Space*.

With the aircraft carrier USS *Intrepid* more than an hour away, the men requested a helicopter pickup. In the meantime, they took their flight suits off to fight the heat. When the helicopter arrived,

Grissom climbed out first since his hatch was clear of water. Young joked it was the first time he ever saw a captain be the first to abandon ship. The helicopter flew Grissom and Young to the *Intrepid*, where they received greetings, congratulations, a physical exam, and warm clothes.

Unlike the controversy and suspicion surrounding his return from space after MR-4, this time Grissom received a proper hero's welcome. He and his family flew to Washington, D.C., and proudly met with President Lyndon B. Johnson. Both he and Young were awarded NASA's Distinguished Service Medal. "For me, personally, the finest award I received was the opportunity for my wife and two sons to meet and shake hands with the President of the United States and Mrs. Johnson and with Vice President [Hubert] Humphrey. It was, I know, a moment that Scott and Mark Grissom will remember for the rest of their lives," Grissom noted in *Gemini!*.

In the months prior to testing *Apollo 1*, Grissom's next scheduled space flight, he began writing his book about the Gemini program, *Gemini!: A Personal Account of Man's Venture into Space*. In the introduction, he explained why he was writing it: "I want

On June 11, 1965, President Lyndon B. Johnson *(fourth from left)* awarded Ed White *(third from left)*, Gus Grissom *(fifth from left)*, and James McDivitt *(sixth from left)* NASA's Distinguished Service Medal. White and McDivitt had successfully completed the *Gemini 4* spaceflight just four days earlier.

Scott and Mark to know just what sort of weird, wonderful enterprise their father was lucky enough to have a part in fulfilling." It was a very lucky thing that Grissom decided to record his thoughts and memories for his sons before the *Apollo 1* mission was underway. The book would prove to be his final words to his family.

CHAPTER 6

AN ASTRONAUT'S LAST RIDE

n the wake of the ticker-tape parades that greeted Gus Grissom and John Young upon their return from space, nine other Gemini missions were successfully undertaken, each putting NASA one step closer to its goal of landing a man on the Moon. With each successive Gemini mission, NASA pushed the spacecraft's performance further as the astronauts continued to set new records. Though the Soviets had achieved the first space walk (an astronaut exited the space capsule to float in space on a tether), NASA soon outdid them with longer and more frequent trips to space. Duration records were set and docking maneuvers performed that paved the way for the upcoming Moon landings of the Apollo missions.

While Grissom had hoped to return to space as a member of a later Gemini mission, the schedule for Gemini quickly filled up. It was clear that things were going by the book and there were few glitches or setbacks, so the program would not need extending. As he had done after his return from the Mercury space flight, Grissom decided to turn his attention to the next stage of NASA's space program. He began to set his sights on the upcoming Apollo program and the development of a three-man Apollo spacecraft that would put a man on the Moon.

Apollo's First Commander

In March 1966, Grissom's hard work and foresight again paid off. NASA formally announced that he would be the commander of the first Apollo mission, which would make him the first astronaut to fly in all three space programs. With the dark shadow of Mercury far behind him, Grissom had evolved into an astronaut's astronaut, a person whose experience, knowledge, and talent NASA relied on again and again to ensure the early success of its space programs. Privately, Grissom was told by fellow astronaut Deke Slayton—the man in charge of scheduling flight crews—that he would be the first astronaut scheduled to set foot on the Moon later in the Apollo program.

On *Apollo 1*, Grissom would be joined by two of NASA's second-generation astronauts, senior pilot Edward White II and pilot Roger B. Chaffee. By the time Grissom was relieved of his Gemini duties, Apollo was well underway, preventing him from digging into the spacecraft design from the beginning, as he had done with Gemini. This may be one of the reasons he was so often unhappy with the construction of the Apollo spacecraft and so outspokenly critical.

A Troubled Program

The Apollo vehicle was much more complex than either the Mercury or Gemini spacecraft. The spacecraft was composed of three connected modules: the command, service, and lunar modules. The command module contained the crew, spacecraft operations systems, and reentry equipment.

A crew compartment heat shield is installed on the command module of Grissom's Apollo spacecraft in April 1966. The early Apollo craft was riddled with mechanical malfunctions and design flaws. Grissom had very little input into the craft's design and never felt confident of the vehicle.

The service module carried most of the craft's supply of oxygen, water, helium, fuel cells, and fuel, and its main propulsion system. The lunar module was the attached craft that was supposed to ferry the astronauts from the main spacecraft to the Moon and back.

Additionally, the contractor involved, North American Aviation, was possibly too busy with too many projects, causing development and delivery problems. The company was already committed to building the *Saturn V* rocket that would propel Apollo toward space.

The Apollo crew actively participated alongside NASA engineers and technicians in the designing and manufacturing reviews of the spacecraft and in the inspections of the vehicle. Grissom often did not like what he was seeing.

When *Spacecraft 0121*, as it was officially named, was delivered to Cape Kennedy (Cape Canaveral was renamed in John F. Kennedy's honor following his death) on August 19, 1966, for review by NASA, it soon became clear that many requested engineering modifications had been left unfinished. Grissom, attending the session at North American Aviation's facility in Downey, California, was angry over the workmanship. The environmental control unit (which controlled cabin air and temperature), for example, leaked, and it needed to be removed, pushing the launch schedule back by weeks.

In the documentary *Moon Shot*, astronaut Walter Cunningham said: "We knew that the spacecraft was, you know, in poor shape relative to

what it ought to be. We felt like we could fly it, but let's face it, it just wasn't as good as it should have been for the job of flying the first manned Apollo mission." Grissom himself told the press: "We've had problems before, but these [with Apollo] have been coming in bushelfuls. Frankly, I think this mission has a pretty damn slim chance of flying its full fourteen days."

The simulator to be used by Grissom's team was outdated because the actual Apollo capsule had received 150 to 200 modifications. The simulator and actual capsule were no longer identical. This made the simulator a poor tool for training purposes. As a result, tests and training were very complicated and confusing. With the December 1966 launch date approaching, Grissom continued to complain about countdowns that were routinely halted due to mechanical glitches and system failures. Deeply frustrated, he finally said, "It's really messy. We want you to go fix it" (as quoted in Charles Murray and Catherine Bly Cox's *Apollo: The Race to the Moon*).

It was not until October 18, 1966, that the first manned flight simulation was conducted.

This is a 1966 portrait of the prime crew for the first manned Apollo flight, taken a year before the tragic accident that would claim their lives. From left are Ed White, Gus Grissom, and Roger Chaffee. A model of the trouble-prone Apollo spacecraft appears in front of them.

Almost immediately, a transistor failed, and the simulation was scrapped. A few days later, *Apollo 1's* backup crew also cancelled their simulation when an oxygen regulator failed. Replacing the regulator cost the team two weeks of preparation time. To add insult to injury, the replacement regulator was also defective, developing leaks that spilled coolant onto electrical wires.

Given the number of bugs that needed to be worked out, NASA had no choice but to postpone the scheduled December 1966 flight of *Apollo 1* until February 1967. Despite all the pressure placed on him during his first two space flights, Grissom had always managed to keep his work and home lives separate. When he was home, he was generally as focused on his wife and children as he was usually on capsule design when at NASA. The frustrations of work usually stayed at work and did not cut into Grissom's valuable time with his family. During the preparations for *Apollo 1*, however, work was going so poorly that he frequently received calls from NASA at home. Betty saw how the pressure affected her husband. As she observed in *Starfall*, "When he was home he normally did not want to be with the space program. He would rather be just messing around with the kids. That was not like Gus. He never brought work problems home with him. But now he was uptight about it."

By January, the command and service modules were finally placed atop the Saturn rocket at Cape Kennedy. The final long-delayed round of simulations was scheduled for January 27, 1967. By then,

The Apollo spacecraft is raised to the top of the gantry at the launchpad in Cape Kennedy, Florida. Once raised, it was placed on top of the *Saturn I* rocket and final tests of the vehicle's systems were conducted. It was during these tests that the fire broke out and killed the *Apollo 1* astronauts.

623 changes had been made to the vehicle since its delivery in August. On January 22, before leaving for Cape Kennedy and one of the final tests of the vehicle's systems, Grissom picked a lemon from a tree in his backyard, claiming he was going to hang it on the spacecraft. When something is described as a "lemon," it means that it is defective. This was his humorous but grim assessment of the quality of

the Apollo vehicle's functioning. It would turn out to be Gus Grissom's last day at home with Betty and the boys.

Fire in the Cockpit

When once asked about the possibility of a serious accident during spaceflight, Gus Grissom took both a philosophical and a practical view. As quoted in John Noble Wilford's *We Reach the Moon*, he replied: "You sort of have to put that out of your mind. There's always a possibility that you can have a catastrophic failure. Of course, this can happen on any flight. It can happen on the last one as well as the first one. So, you just plan as best you can to take care of all these eventualities, and you get a well-trained crew, and you go fly." Grissom was about to confront this very possibility.

On the morning of January 27, the crew climbed to the top of Launch Complex 34 and took an elevator up to the command capsule. They entered the capsule at 1:00 PM and took their assigned positions—Grissom, the flight's commander, on the left;

Chaffee, the rookie pilot, on the right; and White, the senior pilot, in the middle. After the hatch was sealed, the simulation—called a "plugs-out test" (a preflight test of the spacecraft's various systems and instruments)—began and continued until about 1:20 PM. At that time, things were halted when Grissom investigated a strange sour odor coming from his spacesuit's oxygen loops. Nothing was found, and the tests continued as the day wore on slowly.

There were additional holdups and delays, including high oxygen flow levels and faulty communications between the astronauts and the control room. This seemingly endless series of malfunctions and mishaps strained the astronauts' patience until Grissom snapped. According to Murray and Cox's *Apollo: Race to the Moon*, Grissom asked the control room, "How do you expect to get us to the Moon? . . . Get on with it out there." He was frustrated enough that throughout the day he encouraged Deke Slayton—the former Mercury 7 astronaut who now supervised other astronauts—to get into the capsule and see for himself how troubling the problems were.

The tests stretched on into the dinner hour. They were again halted for almost an hour in order to fix another communications failure. At 6:31 PM, just as the tests were about to resume, ground instruments detected another rise in oxygen levels flowing into the spacesuits. Four seconds later, one of the astronauts (probably Roger Chaffee) calmly announced, "Fire, I smell fire" (as reported by the *Apollo 1* summary of events on NASA's Web site). Two seconds after that, Edward White's more urgent voice shouted, "Fire in the cockpit!"

Emergency procedures for escape from the capsule required at least ninety seconds to complete, although the crew had never been able to perform them in the minimum amount of time during practice drills. This fast-moving, intensely hot fire would not give them nearly enough time to escape. Only eighteen seconds separated the moment Ed White's medical sensor detected a change in respiration to the final scream captured on the cockpit recording tape.

Technician Gary Propst was viewing the cockpit from a camera mounted over Ed White's shoulder. He could see the flames and both White

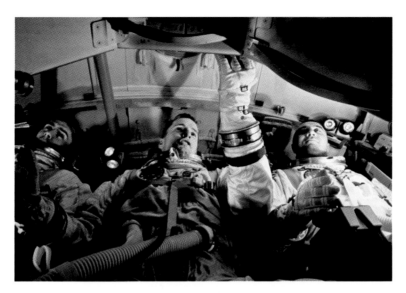

The crew of *Apollo 1* during a practice session in their spacecraft. From left are Roger Chaffee, Ed White, and Gus Grissom. During a similar test, a fire broke out in the capsule, quickly killing all three astronauts. Bottom: The charred remains of the part of the capsule where the fire probably started.

and Grissom trying to release the cabin's hatch bolts. Skip Chauvin, the spacecraft test conductor, heard the astronauts' shouts. He checked a blurry monitor and saw the fire but thought it was outside the craft. When he realized what was happening, he screamed for mission control to cut the power to the craft. Those around Chauvin immediately realized something had gone horribly wrong; he was never known to scream.

Don Babbitt, North American Aviation's pad leader, also heard the astronauts' shouts and then saw flames shoot from the capsule's top, hot enough to singe papers on the desk he was standing beside. He immediately ordered lead technician Jim Gleaves to remove the hatch. While trying to do so, Gleaves was pelted with fire and debris following an explosion in the capsule. This explosion occurred thirty-five seconds after the first report of fire.

Deke Slayton was in another building monitoring events. He heard the astronauts' cries and quickly understood they would have little chance of getting out alive. He called for emergency medics and then placed a call to the Houston Space Center to inform them of what was happening.

Kennedy Space Center was already being sealed off to contain both panic and information and to protect evidence for the inevitable accident investigation.

"Around me in mission control, there was an awful silence," Chris Kraft, head of mission control in Houston, wrote in his memoir, *Flight: My Life in Mission Control.* "Every member of my team sat white-faced and rigid,

Deke Slayton, assistant director for Flight Crew Operations, monitors events at NASA's Mission Control Center at Cape Kennedy.

every ear tuned to the terrible sounds coming from the Cape. We were nine hundred miles [1,448 km] away and helpless."

Despite their best efforts, technicians could not rescue the Apollo astronauts. Flames, heat, and thick black smoke made approaching the capsule impossible at first. Once they were able to reach the capsule, they had to penetrate three layers of metal before they could reach the cabin and its crew—the booster protective cover that shielded the command module from heat and flames during launch, an outer hatch, and the inner hatch. The smoke was so thick that the men could work for only moments at a time until the air cleared. When they finally opened the capsule, a fresh wave of heat and smoke escaped. Once that was cleared, one of the first things they found was Ed White's handprint outlined in ash.

Firefighters arrived three minutes after the hatch was opened, and doctors a few minutes later. In the moments that followed the opening of the capsule, firefighters needed to turn their attention to containing the fire that was spreading from level A8 to A7 on the launch tower, near the Saturn rocket itself. Although it did not yet contain any fuel, it could still combust, setting the entire launch service structure on fire. Twenty-seven technicians and rescuers had to be treated for smoke-related illnesses.

It took seven hours after the fire was extinguished before the astronauts' bodies could be removed from the capsule. Part of the delay was a result of the fire's heat melting portions of the flight suits to the astronauts' seats. It was later determined

An accident investigator studies the badly burnt interior of the *Apollo 1* spacecraft for clues that would explain the cause of the fire. It was eventually determined that an electrical spark from a frayed wire ignited the pure oxygen environment of the capsule, resulting in the rapid and intense fire.

that the flight suits protected the men from the flames, but the pure oxygen escaping into the capsule ignited, suffocating them. The heat inside the capsule had risen as high as 1400°F (760° Celsius). Grissom was found to have burns on his legs while White had burns on his back. Chaffee was the only astronaut still strapped into his seat. The medical analysis panel determined that the astronauts had

THE REPORT'S FINDINGS

A three-month-long review involving twenty-one separate investigative panels followed the tragic accident. The end result was a 3,000-page report that was harshly self-critical. NASA went so far as to review their entire contractor bidding process, step-by-step approvals, astronaut training, ground crew training, and several other major planning and development procedures. Scott Simpkinson, the engineer in charge of disassembling the remains of the capsule, and editor of the *Report of the Apollo 204 Review Board*, identified the following likely sequence of events leading up to the fire (*Apollo 204* was the original name of the mission; it was rechristened *Apollo 1* after the accident in tribute to Grissom, White, and Chaffee):

1. A compartment full of lithium hydroxide (which removes carbon dioxide from the capsule so the cabin air remains breathable) had a door with a sharp edge.

2. The door opened into the environmental control unit (ECU). Just underneath the ECU, a cable was wedged against the door. Each time the door closed, it rubbed against the cable, fraying it in one section and exposing two tiny sections of wire.

3. A brief electrical spark passed between these wires. Alone, the spark was not enough to ignite the pure oxygen atmosphere. Below the exposed wires, however, ran aluminum tubing. Inside the tubing was glycol cooling liquid, which has flammable fumes. These fumes were rising from a crack in a section of the aluminum tubing that was bent at a 90-degree angle.

4. Nearby was some nylon netting that was hanging lower than recommended. The wires' spark ignited the glycol fumes, which caught on the netting, and a fire spread rapidly through the capsule, intensifying when it ignited the pure oxygen streaming through the cabin.

lost consciousness within fifteen to thirty seconds after the first suit began burning. The astronauts had died of carbon monoxide poisoning and burns.

At their Houston home, Betty Grissom heard the news on television before being called by NASA. Rene Carpenter, wife of Mercury 7 astronaut Scott Carpenter, was the first astronaut wife to arrive at the Grissom home, and she stayed by Betty's side during the following days. She even saw to it that Mark and Scott got some attention while funeral preparations were being made.

Betty asked Chris Kraft, Johnson Space Center director Bob Gilruth, and NASA mission director Walt Williams to be pallbearers. They flew to Arlington, Virginia, where Grissom and Chaffee were to be laid to rest. The night before the funeral, U.S. vice president Hubert Humphrey visited the widows and their families and was such a comfort that he stayed until 2:00 AM.

"But that morning," Kraft remembered in *Flight*, "walking behind the caisson carrying Gus Grissom in a casket, was something I never wanted to do again. The cold, gusty, and penetrating day made our task all the more uncomfortable. The eulogies, military regalia, rifle salutes, and the bugler playing Taps are familiar to everyone. But when that caisson carried my friend, and I had this aching feeling of responsibility for putting him there, it made me not only cry, but resolve that it would never happen again."

Apollo Goes On

If the account contained within the accident report is accurate, the tragedy of *Apollo 1* was a series of minor mishaps, each based upon sloppy or incorrect capsule design, that created a devastating and deadly chain reaction. The wiring was placed in an unsafe area near a sharp door edge, modifications had moved the aluminum tubing too close to the electrical wires, the netting was not up to specification and hanging too low, and there was an unusually high amount of flammable Velcro in the cabin. In addition, all safety procedures were not being followed during the series of tests leading up to the fire. Finally, due to all the design changes made over the preceding months to address the many system malfunctions that so

Though begun in fiery tragedy, the Apollo space program eventually triumphed. On July 20, 1969, Neil Armstrong and Buzz Aldrin touched down upon the lunar surface and became the first humans ever to walk on the Moon during the *Apollo 11* spaceflight. Aldrin is seen here after hoisting the American flag.

angered Grissom, a high percentage of the craft no longer matched the original design and safety controls. There had been so much fiddling around to make things work, that corners may have been cut and potential problems overlooked.

There was no question that Apollo would continue, despite the tragedy and the first loss of life in the American space program. In the wake of the accident, NASA made certain the Apollo spacecraft would be the safest, most reliable vehicle it was possible to make. *Apollo 1*'s tragedy gave way to a series of both unmanned and manned Apollo missions that rigorously tested the rockets, command modules, lunar landers, and other technology and machinery necessary to complete a successful Moon shot.

Finally, on July 20, 1969, the Apollo program, to which Grissom, White, and Chaffee sacrificed their lives, put a man on the Moon. During *Apollo 11*, Neil A. Armstrong and Buzz Aldrin said good-bye to their partner Michael Collins, climbed into the lunar module, separated from the command module (Collins would continue to orbit overhead), and flew to the lunar surface. People all over the world stopped what they were doing that day to tune into television to watch Armstrong climb down from the lunar module. He became the first human in history to set foot on the Moon, saying, "That's one small step for man, one giant leap for mankind." Human beings had left Earth's atmosphere behind, traveled through outer space, and reached the Moon. The deaths of the *Apollo 1* astronauts had not been in vain.

In the wake of *Apollo 11*'s success, American astronauts returned to the Moon four more times. The last Moon shot occurred during *Apollo 17* in December 1972. An American has not returned to the Moon since. "I hate it that Gus is gone," Betty is quoted as saying by IndianaHistory.org. "But I guess the [Apollo] program was worth it. He wouldn't have had it any other way."

CONCLUSION

A PIONEER'S LEGACY

The first American deaths related to the space program slowed but did not stop America's quest for outer space. To this day, their efforts are remembered. Immediately after Grissom's death, on May 12, 1968, Bunker Hill AFB in north-central Indiana was renamed Grissom AFB in the astronaut's honor. When the base became a reserve facility in 1994, the name was changed to Grissom Air Reserve Base.

The people of Mitchell, Indiana, did not forget Grissom's sacrifice, either. Governor Edgar D. Whitcomb dedicated the Virgil I. "Gus" Grissom State Memorial, near Spring Mill State Park near Grissom's hometown.

In the park, Grissom's Gemini capsule, spacesuit, and other items are displayed. Next to Mitchell's city hall stands a forty-four-foot (13 m) limestone monument carved in the shape of the Gemini spacecraft.

Don Caudell, who was responsible for raising funds for the monument, told IndianaHistory.org, "[Grissom] came from the ground up and, by his own efforts, he got to a place where people hadn't been before. That's what made him special." He went on to tell the Associated Press, "We didn't build it because he got killed. We built it because of his life. He made it, and he didn't have anybody pulling for him. He did it on his own."

On anniversary dates, the press usually finds something new to report about Grissom's career. On the thirtieth anniversary of the *Apollo 1* tragedy, the Associated Press profiled his brother Norman, who had continued to live in Mitchell, Indiana. On that awful day in 1967, while covering a high school basketball game in nearby Salem for the *Mitchell Tribune*, "a family friend called and told me that there had been, you know, I forget how he phrased it. A tragedy . . . We're sincerely proud of

Gus Grissom's body is carried in a flag-covered casket to Arlington National Cemetery for burial services on January 31, 1967. In procession to the right are fellow Mercury 7 astronauts John Glenn, Gordon Cooper, Alan Shepard, and Scott Carpenter.

what he did and the legacy he left. I'm not bashful about talking to people about it."

On the thirty-fourth anniversary of the *Apollo 1* disaster, the original artwork for a new mission patch was presented to Betty Grissom during a ceremony. The mission patch commemorated Grissom, with "GUS" embroidered at the top in gold, surrounded by black, depicting the black and

 A monument to Gus Grissom stands in Spring Mill State Park, near his hometown of Mitchell, Indiana. It is a 44-foot (13 m) limestone statue carved in the shape of the rocket used on Grissom's Gemini mission. Grissom's Gemini capsule, spacesuit, and other items are also on display nearby.

gold colors of the Third Space Launch Squadron (the group that conducted launch operations for the Titan rockets used in the Gemini program). The black border signifies the blackness of space, the final frontier. Blue is for the sky through which the astronauts fly, and green represents Earth and all the people who support the launch program. Years after his death and even longer after his first trip to space aboard *Mercury-Redstone 4*, Grissom was finally achieving the recognition and honor he deserved.

Gus Grissom's legacy shines bright. A true space pioneer, he gladly gave his time and, ultimately, his life to the space program because he truly believed in his job. Had he been born 150 years earlier, he once said, he would likely have been among the pioneers to explore the West. It was in his nature to strive toward the unknown and the unseen, to test the boundaries of human experience. Perhaps more than anything else, that is Gus Grissom's true legacy to people all over the world.

GLOSSARY

abort To cancel a mission once it has begun.

Apollo space program The third generation of space capsules flown by NASA; the successful goal of the Apollo program was to launch a manned spacecraft that would orbit and land on the Moon.

attitude The position of a spacecraft as determined by the relation of its axes to some frame of reference, usually Earth's surface.

axis Any of three straight lines, the first running through the center of an object lengthwise, the second at right angles to the first line, and the third perpendicular to the first two at their point of intersection.

booster An engine that assists a spacecraft's main propulsion, or thrusting, system.

capsule A small pressurized cabin that houses the astronauts during spaceflight.

explosive bolts Bolts surrounded with an explosive charge that can be blown open by an electrical charge.

flotation collar A collar inflated around a spacecraft used to keep the craft upright in water.

Gemini space program The second stage of space exploration by NASA; Gemini space capsules held two people.

launchpad The load-bearing base or platform from which a rocket vehicle is launched.

Mercury space program The first manned space missions organized by NASA and flown by the Mercury 7—the first group of American astronauts in history.

module A self-contained unit of a spacecraft, which serves as one of the building blocks of the overall structure.

NASA The National Aeronautics and Space Administration, founded in 1958 to promote space exploration, technology, and scientific research.

orbit To revolve around or circle something. A spacecraft is inserted into a controlled orbit around a planet like Earth or any other large celestial body, like the Moon, using gravity and its own propulsion systems.

pitch The up-and-down movement of an airplane or spacecraft.

rendezvous and docking Complicated maneuvers in space that allow separate spacecraft to join together.

roll A complete side-to-side revolution of an airplane or spacecraft.

thrust The propulsive force created by an aircraft engine or rocket engine.

weightlessness The floating sensation astronauts experience when they leave Earth's field of gravity, as if their bodies weighed nothing. The Moon has a gravitational field with a pull one-sixth the size of Earth's; astronauts aren't weightless on the Moon, but they feel and move like they weigh only one-sixth as much as they normally do.

yaw The side-to-side movement of an airplane or spacecraft.

FOR MORE INFORMATION

American Astronautical Society
6352 Rolling Mill Place, Suite 102
Springfield, VA 22152-2354
(703) 866-0020
Web site: http://www.astronautical.org

Jet Propulsion Laboratory
Public Services Office
Mail Stop 186-113
4800 Oak Grove Drive
Pasadena, CA 91109
(818) 354-9314
Web site: http://www.jpl.nasa.gov

Johnson Space Center
Visitors Center
1601 NASA Road 1

Houston, TX 77058
(281) 244-2100
Web site: http://www.jsc.nasa.gov

Kennedy Space Center Visitor Complex
Mail Code: DNPS
Kennedy Space Center, FL 32899
(321) 449-4444
Web site: http://www.kennedyspacecenter.com

NASA Headquarters
Information Center
Washington, DC 20546-0001
(202) 358-0000
Web site: http://www.nasa.gov

National Air and Space Museum
Seventh Street and Independence Avenue SW
Washington, DC 20560
(202) 357-2700
Web site: http://www.nasm.si.edu

Space Policy Institute
1957 E Street NW, Suite 403
Washington, DC 20052
(202) 994-7292
Web site: http://www.gwu.edu/~spi

U.S. Space Camp
P.O. Box 070015
Huntsville, AL 35807-7015
(800) 533-7281
(256) 721-7150
Web site: http://www.spacecamp.com

Web Sites

Due to the changing nature of Internet links, the
Rosen Publishing Group, Inc., has developed an
online list of Web sites related to the subject of this
book. This site is updated regularly. Please use this
link to access the list:

http://www.rosenlinks.com/lasb/ggri

FOR FURTHER READING

Cole, Michael D. *Astronauts: Training for Space.*
Springfield, NJ: Enslow Publishers, 1999.

Crocker, Chris. *Great American Astronauts.* New
York: Franklin Watts, 1988.

Deedrick, Tami. *Astronauts.* Mankato, MN: Bridgestone
Books, 1998.

Glatzer, Jenna. *The Exploration of the Moon: How
American Astronauts Traveled 240,000 Miles to the
Moon and Back, and the Fascinating Things They
Found There.* Vaughn, Ontario: Mason Crest
Publishers, 2002.

Hayhurst, Chris. *Astronauts: Life Exploring Outer
Space.* New York: The Rosen Publishing Group,
Inc., 2001.

Kerrod, Robin. *The Children's Space Atlas: A Voyage
of Discovery for Young Astronauts.* Brookfield, CT:
Millbrook Press Trade, 1993.

Lassieur, Allison. *Astronauts*. Danbury, CT: Children's Press, 2000.

Sipiera, Diane M., and Paul P. Sipiera. *Project Mercury*. Danbury, CT: Children's Press, 1998.

Thompson, Kim M. *Space: Learning About Gravity, Space Travel, and Famous Astronauts*. Akron, OH: Twin Sisters Productions, 2001.

Wolfe, Tom. *The Right Stuff*. New York: Bantam Doubleday Dell, 2001.

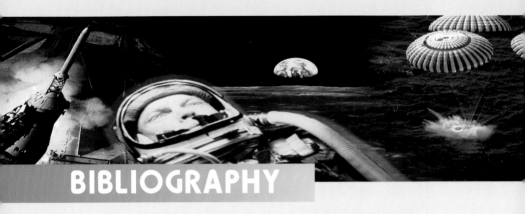

BIBLIOGRAPHY

Bond, Peter. *Heroes in Space: From Gagarin to Challenger.* Oxford, England: Basil Blackwell Ltd., 1987.

Bonke, Jim. "Gus Grissom Didn't Sink Liberty Bell 7." Space.com. June 17, 2000. Retrieved July 2003 (http://www.space.com/missionlaunches/missions/liberty_bell_000617.html).

Burrows, William E. *The Infinite Journey: Eyewitness Accounts of NASA and the Age of Space.* New York: Discovery Books, 2000.

Carpenter, Scott, et. al. *We Seven.* New York: Simon & Schuster, 1962.

Carpenter, Scott, and Kris Stoever. *For Spacious Skies.* New York: Harcourt, Inc., 2003.

Collins, Michael. *Lift Off: The Story of America's Adventure in Space.* New York: Groce Press, 1988.

Grissom, Virgil I. *Gemini!* New York: Macmillan, 1968.

Grissom, Betty, and Henry Still. *Starfall*. New York: Thomas Y. Crowell Company, 1974.

"In Search of Liberty Bell 7." DiscoveryChannel.com. 2000. Retrieved 2003 (http://discovery.com/exp/libertybell7/libertybell7.html.

Kraft, Chris. *Flight: My Life in Mission Control*. New York: Dutton, 2001.

Kranz, Gene. *Failure Is Not an Option: Mission Control from Mercury to Apollo 13 and Beyond*. New York: Simon & Schuster, 2000.

Life magazine. *Project Mercury*. New York: Simon & Schuster, 1964.

Murray, Charles, and Catherine Bly Cox. *Apollo: The Race to the Moon*. New York: Simon & Schuster, 1989.

Shepard, Alan, Deke Slayton, Jay Barbree, and Howard Benedict. *Moon Shot: The Inside Story of America's Race to the Moon*. Paducah, KY: Turner Publishing, 1994.

Slayton, Donald, with Michael Cassutt. *Deke!: U.S. Manned Space: From Mercury to the Shuttle*. New York: Tom Doherty Associates, Inc., 1994.

Stott, Carole. *Space Exploration*. New York: Alfred A. Knopf, 1997.

INDEX

A

Aldrin, Buzz, 93
Apollo program, 6–7, 36, 45, 58,
    65, 69, 71, 72, 73–76, 79, 85,
    91, 92–93, 94
Apollo 1, 69, 70, 73, 75, 76–79,
    80–82, 88–89, 91–92, 93,
    96–97
  fire aboard, 82–87
  investigation into fire, 88–89
Apollo 11, 93, 94
Apollo 13, 55
Apollo 17, 94
Armstrong, Neil, 93

C

Carpenter, Malcolm Scott, 32, 90
Chaffee, Roger B., 73, 80, 82, 87,
    88, 90, 93
Cold War, 15–17, 26
Collins, Michael, 93
Cooper, Gordon, 23

F

Freedom 7, 37

G

Gagarin, Yuri, 35
Gemini program, 6, 36, 58, 59–65,
    71–72, 73, 96, 99
Gemini 2, 65
Gemini 3, 62, 65–68
Glenn, John, 32
Grissom, Betty (nee Moore), 10,
    11, 12–13, 17–18, 23, 52, 69,
    78, 80, 90, 94, 97
Grissom, Gus (Virgil Ivan),
  in armed forces, 10–12, 17–21
  astronaut training of, 30–35
  childhood of, 8–10
  in college, 12–14
  death of, 6, 7, 87–90, 95, 99
  early jobs held, 9–10, 12, 13
  as fighter pilot, 6, 18–20
  and Gemini program, 60–61,
    63–65
  and *Liberty Bell* 7 controversy,
    48–57, 69
  as NASA candidate, 27–29, 30–31
  parents of, 8–9, 62

siblings of, 8, 96–97
space flights of, 38, 39, 41–48
as test pilot, 6, 21–23
Grissom Air Force Base, 95

K

Kansas Cosmosphere and Space
  Center, 54–55
Kennedy, John F., 7, 51
Korean War, 16, 18–20

L

Liberty Bell 7, 41, 43, 44, 48–52, 53,
  54–55, 56, 59, 62, 63
  loss of, 48–52, 53, 56
  recovery of, 54–55

M

Mercury program, 18, 23, 25, 27,
  28, 32–33, 35, 36, 37, 57, 59,
  61, 64, 72, 73
Mercury-Redstone 3 (MR-3), 37, 45
Mercury-Redstone 4 (MR-4), 38, 40,
  43, 52, 57, 69, 72, 99
Mercury 7 astronauts, 6, 7, 25,
  32–33, 63, 90
Molly Brown, 62, 67
Moon, 6, 7, 36, 39, 45, 58, 65, 66,
  71, 72, 73, 74, 81
  landing on the, 93–94

N

National Aeronautics and Space
  Administration (NASA), 23,
  27–29, 33, 35, 37, 38, 41, 45,

47, 52, 53, 57–58, 62, 63,
  65–66, 69, 71, 72, 75, 77–78,
  82, 88, 90, 92, 93

S

Schirra, Walter Jr., 32–33, 53–56, 60
Shepard, Alan Jr., 33, 35, 37–38,
  39, 45
Slayton, Donald "Deke," 33, 63, 73,
  81, 84
Soviet Union, 15–16, 17, 18, 23–26,
  35, 37, 38, 71
Sputnik, 23–26

T

test pilots, 17, 21, 24–25, 27, 28, 64

U

U.S. Air Force, 17, 21–23, 28, 32, 33

V

Virgil I. "Gus" Grissom State
  Memorial, 95–96
Vostok 1, 35, 37

W

White II, Edward, 73, 80, 82, 86,
  87, 88, 93
Wright-Patterson Air Force Base,
  21–23, 30

Y

Yeager, Chuck, 24–25
Young, John W., 63–65, 67, 69, 71

About the Author

Robert Greenberger currently works as a senior editor at DC Comics. Additionally, he is a freelance writer experienced in a diverse range of subject matter. Most frequently, he writes fiction in the *Star Trek* universe, but also has written biographies for young adults, including books on Ponce de Leon and Lou Gehrig. He makes his home in Connecticut with his wife, Deb, and children, Katie and Robbie.

Photo Credits

Cover, pp. 1, 4–5, 31, 32, 42, 46, 49, 50, 60, 61, 64, 66, 68, 74, 77, 79, 85, 92 courtesy of NASA; pp. 9, 55, 83, 87 © AP/Wide World Photos; p. 13 courtesy of Special Collections, Purdue University Libraries; p. 16 © Hulton/Getty/Archive/Getty Images; pp. 19, 22 (right), 25, 26, 34, 44, 53, 57, 70, 97 © Bettmann/Corbis; p. 22 (left) © Hulton-Deutsch Collection/Corbis; p. 39 © Museum of Flight/Corbis; p. 98 © James H. Gerard.

Designer: Les Kanturek